TEAM SPIRIT

SMART BOOKS FOR YOUNG FANS

THE DETROIT RED WINGS

BY
MARK STEWART

CONTENT CONSULTANT
DENIS GIBBONS
SOCIETY FOR INTERNATIONAL HOCKEY RESEARCH

NORWOOD HOUSE PRESS
CHICAGO, ILLINOIS

Norwood House Press
P.O. Box 316598
Chicago, Illinois 60631

For information regarding Norwood House Press, please visit our website at:
www.norwoodhousepress.com or call 866-565-2900.

All photos courtesy of Associated Press except the following:
Hamilton Gum (6), Beckett Publications (7), Getty Images (8, 10, 12, 18, 19, 25, 27, 31, 32),
Black Book Partners (9), Hockey Illustrated, Inc. (15, 38, 39),
Bee Hive Golden Corn Syrup/Cargill, Inc. (16, 34 left), McDiarmid/Cartophilium (17),
Sport Revue Enr. (21), The Hockey News (23, 41), Author's Collection (33, 43, 45),
Topps, Inc. (34 right, 35 top left), The Upper Deck Company (35 bottom, 42 top),
TIME Inc./Sports Illustrated for Kids (35 top right), Complete Sports Publications (36), IKEA (37),
O-Pee-Chee Ltd. (40), Parkhurst Products (42 bottom).
Cover Photo: Cal Sport Media via AP Images

The memorabilia and artifacts pictured in this book are presented for educational and informational purposes,
and come from the collection of the author.

Editor: Mike Kennedy
Designer: Ron Jaffe
Project Management: Black Book Partners, LLC.
Special thanks to Topps, Inc.

Library of Congress Cataloging-in-Publication Data

Stewart, Mark, 1960 July 7-
  The Detroit Red Wings / by Mark Stewart.
      pages cm. -- (Team spirit)
  Includes bibliographical references and index.
  Summary: "A revised Team Spirit Hockey edition featuring the Detroit Red
Wings that chronicles the history and accomplishments of the team. Includes
access to the Team Spirit website which provides additional information and
photos"-- Provided by publisher.
  ISBN 978-1-59953-619-4 (library edition : alk. paper) -- ISBN
978-1-60357-627-7 (ebook) 1. Detroit Red Wings (Hockey
team)--History--Juvenile literature. I. Title.
  GV848.D47S74 2014
  796.962'640977434--dc23
                                              2013034892

Manufactured in the United States of America in Stevens Point, Wisconsin.
239N—012014

COVER PHOTO: Goalie Jimmy Howard is congratulated after a big win during
the 2012–13 season.

TABLE OF CONTENTS

ABOUT OUR GLOSSARY

In this book, there may be several words that you are reading for the first time. Some are sports words, some are new vocabulary words, and some are familiar words that are used in an unusual way. All of these words are defined on page 46. Throughout the book, sports words appear in **bold type**. Regular vocabulary words appear in ***bold italic type***.

MEET THE RED WINGS

In the **National Hockey League (NHL)**, only one team a year can claim that it's the best. And that team takes home the trophy to prove it—the **Stanley Cup**. Look at that trophy carefully, and you'll see the Detroit Red Wings listed as champions over 10 times. No team from the United States has won the trophy more often.

Every season for nearly 90 years, the "Wings" have taken the ice hoping to add their names to the Stanley Cup one more time. It takes hard work, talent, teamwork, and a little luck. When the Red Wings have put all those pieces together, they have accomplished great things.

This book tells the story of the Red Wings. During the team's proud history, Detroit fans have cheered for legendary scorers and speedy skaters. They have welcomed stars from all over the world. And they have seen the Wings win the Stanley Cup—again and again and again.

Coach Mike Babcock scans the ice as Joakim Andersson and Henrik Zetterberg cheer on their teammates.

During the early years of the NHL, the league's future was uncertain. Canadian fans loved hockey, but the country's population was too small to support the NHL. Would fans in big American cities pay to watch hockey? The NHL hoped so. During the 1920s, the league formed several new teams in the U.S., including one in Detroit, Michigan.

EBBIE GOODFELLOW

That team actually got its start as the Victoria Cougars, in the **Western Hockey League (WHL)**. In 1925 and 1926, Victoria played for the Stanley Cup—and won it once! A group of investors soon bought the Cougars and moved the team to Detroit. In 1927, Jack Adams was hired to run the club. He would stay in that position for more than three *decades*.

After four seasons as the Cougars, Adams changed the team name to the Falcons. That lasted until 1932, when James Norris bought the club. He changed the name to Red Wings. During the 1930s, Detroit finished first in its **division** three times. The Wings won the

Stanley Cup in 1936 and 1937. Detroit's top player was Ebbie Goodfellow, a defenseman who skated and shot like a forward. Other leaders during the 1930s included Herbie Lewis, Larry Aurie, and Marty Barry.

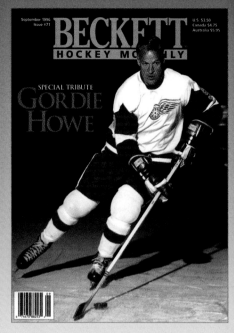

A new group of stars led Detroit into the 1940s, including Sid Abel, Syd Howe, Jack Stewart, Bill Quackenbush, and Johnny Mowers. They delivered a third Stanley Cup to Detroit in 1943. In the years after *World War II*, Abel teamed with a pair of tough and talented young superstars—Ted Lindsay, and Gordie Howe—on the high-scoring "Production **Line**." This threesome led the Red Wings to three more Stanley Cups in the early 1950s. Their teammates included center Alex Delvecchio, defensemen Red Kelly and Leo Reise Jr., and goalie Terry Sawchuk.

By the 1960s, only Howe, Delvecchio, and Sawchuk remained from those great teams. They formed the heart of a fantastic new squad. From 1961 to 1966, Detroit made it to the **Stanley Cup Finals** four times. Unfortunately, the Red Wings fell short of the title each year, despite the contributions of hard-nosed players such as Norm Ullman, Bill Gadsby, Marcel Pronovost, and Roger Crozier.

LEFT: Ebbie Goodfellow led Detroit to two Stanley Cups in the 1930s.
ABOVE: Gordie Howe was the toughest player in team history.

In the 1970s and 1980s, the Red Wings struggled for the first time in team history. They had some bad luck, but they also made some poor decisions. Mickey Redmond was an amazing scorer, but he hurt his back. Marcel Dionne set a record for most points (goals plus **assists**) by a **rookie**, but he was traded away. Reed Larson, a defenseman with a great slapshot, was also traded. John Ogrodnick was one of the top left wings in the NHL, but the team failed to surround him with good players.

Detroit's luck began to change after it **drafted** Steve Yzerman in 1983. Yzerman was an elegant and creative player who could score at any time. In 1988–89, he led the NHL in goals and assists. However, it was when Yzerman began focusing his efforts on defense in the early 1990s that the Red Wings became a championship *contender*.

At the time, many hockey stars from Russia were coming to the NHL. The Red Wings added Slava Fetisov, Slava Kozlov, Igor Larionov, Vladimir Konstantinov, and Sergei Fedorov. Few forwards were better than Fedorov. He had a very hard slapshot and seemed to be everywhere on the ice at once.

LEFT: After Steve Yzerman arrived in Detroit, the Wings became champions again.   **ABOVE**: Sergei Fedorov was one of many Russian stars who played for Detroit in the 1990s.

The Wings added even more talented stars and **veterans** over the next few years, including goalie Mike Vernon and defensemen Nicklas Lidstrom and Larry Murphy. In 1996–97, Detroit won the Stanley Cup for the first time in 42 seasons, under coach Scotty Bowman. In 1997–98, Bowman led the Wings to the NHL title again. Bowman still had Lidstrom, Yzerman, Fedorov, and Larionov in his lineup four years later when Detroit won the Stanley Cup for the 10th time.

In the years after the 2002 championship, many of Detroit's veterans left the team or retired. So did Bowman. Many questioned whether the Red Wings could win with a new coach and young players. The Wings rebuilt around Lidstrom, who had become the NHL's top defenseman. They also brought back two of their Stanley Cup-winning goalies, Chris Osgood and Dominik Hasek. The difference-makers, however, were the exciting young stars Detroit put on the ice.

Pavel Datsyuk, Henrik Zetterberg, Johan Franzen, Niklas Kronwall, Jiri Hudler, and Jimmy Howard gave Detroit fans plenty to cheer about during the 2007–08 season. Coach Mike Babcock guided the Red Wings to a league-leading 54 victories. Detroit rolled through the **playoffs** and defeated the Pittsburgh Penguins in the Stanley Cup Finals to win the 11th championship in team history.

Zetterberg and Datsyuk continued to lead the Wings to victory. Zetterberg blasted shots from every angle and threw defenses into a panic. Datsyuk became one of the NHL's most respected players. He won the Selke Trophy as the top defensive forward three times, and the Lady Byng Trophy for sportsmanship four times. In 2011–12, Lidstrom finally hung up his skates after two decades. It was the end of an amazing *era* in Detroit, but the Red Wings barely missed a beat. In 2012–13, the Wings had their 23rd winning season in a row.

LEFT: Dominik Hasek makes a save.
ABOVE: Pavel Datsyuk and Nicklas Lidstrom talk about their gameplan.

HOME ICE

From 1927 to 1979, the Red Wings played in the Olympia, which fans nicknamed the "Big Old Red Barn." By the 1970s, however, Detroit's owners wanted a new home. The city made them a deal they could not refuse—a new downtown arena with an inexpensive 30-year contract.

Two days after Christmas in 1979, the Wings moved into their beautiful new home, Joe Louis Arena. It was named after a famous boxer who grew up in Detroit. After 30 years, the team and the city decided that a new building was needed. It would be part of a new plan to remake Detroit's downtown area.

BY THE NUMBERS

- The team's arena has 19,275 seats for hockey.
- The arena cost $57 million to build in the 1970s.
- The Wings defeated the St. Louis Blues 3–2 in the first NHL game played at Joe Louis Arena.

Banners celebrating Detroit's championships hang from the ceiling of Joe Louis Arena.

13

DRESSED FOR SUCCESS

The Red Wings got their name in 1932 from their new owner, James Norris. He also designed the team's *logo*, which features a "flying" wheel. Norris got the idea from an old hockey team called the Winged Wheelers. He hoped the new logo would draw new fans to the arena. Back then, thousands of people in Michigan built cars for a living. The flying wheel reminded them of the pride they had in their jobs.

Detroit's colors have been red and white since the team's first season. The Red Wings usually wear red sweaters for home games and white ones for games on the road. The team also wore these colors as the Cougars and the Falcons. From time to time, the Red Wings wear a third uniform that reminds fans of the club's earliest years. It is reserved for special occasions only.

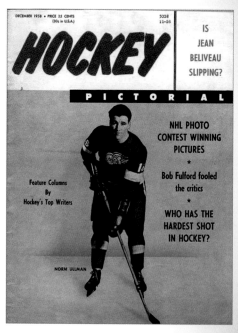

DECEMBER 1958 • PRICE 25 CENTS
(30c in U.S.A.)
5208
11-08

HOCKEY

PICTORIAL

Feature Columns By Hockey's Top Writers

NORM ULLMAN

IS JEAN BELIVEAU SLIPPING?

NHL PHOTO CONTEST WINNING PICTURES
★
Bob Fulford fooled the critics
★
WHO HAS THE HARDEST SHOT IN HOCKEY?

LEFT: Niklas Kronwall wears the team's away uniform during the 2012–13 season. **ABOVE**: Norm Ullman models Detroit's uniform on this magazine cover from the 1950s.

15

The Red Wings captured their first two Stanley Cups in back-to-back seasons. They won the championship for the first time in 1936. Goalie Norm Smith led them to victory over the Toronto Maple Leafs. One year later, they played the New York Rangers in the Stanley Cup Finals. Smith was injured, but Earl Robertson stepped in as his replacement. Detroit became the first team from the United States to take the Stanley Cup two years in a row.

Johnny Mowers

The Wings made it to the Stanley Cup Finals six times during the 1940s, but they won the championship just once. After losing in the finals in 1941 and 1942, the Wings returned in 1943, this time against the Boston Bruins. Detroit swept Boston in four games. Mud Bruneteau and Don Grosso each scored a **hat trick** in the series, and goalie Johnny Mowers **shut out** the Bruins in the final two games.

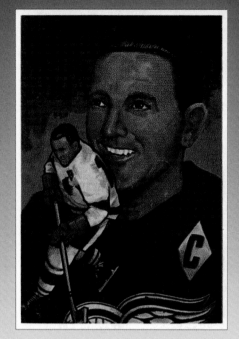

The 1949–50 season was an amazing one for the Red Wings. By this time, the line of Ted Lindsay, Sid Abel, and Gordie Howe was being called the best ever. They were the top three finishers in the NHL scoring race. The Rangers were not impressed. They battled Detroit in seven thrilling games for the Stanley Cup. The decisive contest went into **overtime**. In the second extra period, George Gee of the Red Wings slipped a pass from behind the net to teammate Pete Babando. He whacked the puck through a forest of players and into the goal for a 4–3 victory. It was the first time a Game 7 of the Stanley Cup Finals was won in overtime.

Two years later, the Red Wings had a hot young goalie named Terry Sawchuk. He backed up a great defense led by Red Kelly. Detroit finished the season with the league's best record, and then swept through the playoffs without losing a game. In the Stanley Cup Finals, they rolled over the Montreal Canadiens in four games. Some fans say this was the best Detroit team ever.

The Red Wings won the Stanley Cup again in 1954. This time they needed seven games to beat the Canadiens. The last game went into overtime. Detroit won on a surprising play. Tony Leswick flipped the puck toward the Montreal goal, and it found its way into the net after bouncing off a defenseman.

A year later, the Wings and Canadiens met again for the championship. Again the series lasted seven games. Detroit won with strong goaltending from Sawchuk and excellent offense by Howe and Alex Delvecchio. Howe's 12 points in the finals set a record.

Detroit fans believed there would be many more Stanley Cups in the team's future. No one could have imagined it would take 42 years to win the next one. For the 1996–97 season, the Red Wings put together a team of modern stars that liked to play old-time hockey. Steve Yzerman, Sergei Fedorov, Igor Larionov, and Brendan Shanahan led Detroit to a sweep of the Philadelphia Flyers. Mike Vernon was nearly unbeatable in the net for the Wings.

One year later, Chris Osgood was Detroit's goalie. He was just as good in the playoffs as Vernon had been the year before. The Red Wings swept the Washington Capitals in four games to claim their ninth Stanley Cup.

The Wings won the Stanley Cup again in 2002. Yzerman, Fedorov, and Shanahan were joined by four more "old-timers"—Brett Hull, Dominik Hasek, Chris Chelios, and Luc Robitaille. Hull scored 10 goals in the playoffs, and Detroit beat the Carolina Hurricanes in the Stanley Cup Finals. By 2007–08, a new *generation* had taken over for the Red Wings. Young stars Henrik Zetterberg, Pavel Datsyuk, Johan Franzen, and Niklas Kronwall followed the lead of Nicklas Lidstrom—a hero of past championships. Detroit defeated the Pittsburgh Penguins in six games to capture its 11th Stanley Cup.

LEFT: Igor Larionov raises the Stanley Cup in 1997.   **ABOVE**: Chris Chelios and Henrik Zetterberg celebrate Detroit's 11th championship.

GO-TO GUYS

To be a true star in the NHL, you need more than a great slapshot. You have to be a "go-to guy"—someone teammates trust to make the winning play when the seconds are ticking away in a big game. Red Wings fans have had a lot to cheer about over the years, including these great stars.

THE PIONEERS

SID ABEL   Left Wing/Center

• Born: 2/22/1918   • Died: 2/8/2000   • Played for Team: 1938–39 to 1951–52

Sid Abel was named team captain at age 24. He was a star as a left wing and then as a center. Abel was the leader of Detroit's "Production Line." He won the Hart Trophy as the NHL's **Most Valuable Player (MVP)** in 1948–49.

TED LINDSAY   Left Wing

• Born: 7/29/1925   • Played for Team: 1944–45 to 1956–57 & 1964–65

Ted Lindsay stood only 5′ 8″ and weighed just 160 pounds, but he was pure muscle and energy. His nickname was "Terrible Ted" because of his aggressive style on the ice. He won the Art Ross Trophy as the NHL's top scorer in 1949–50.

GORDIE HOWE   Right Wing

- BORN: 3/31/1928
- PLAYED FOR TEAM: 1946–47 TO 1970–71

Gordie Howe was almost impossible to stop on the ice. He had a hard, accurate shot, and no one was better at protecting the puck. When Howe left the Wings, he was the NHL's all-time leader with 786 goals.

RED KELLY   Defenseman

- BORN: 7/9/1927
- PLAYED FOR TEAM: 1947–48 TO 1959–60

Red Kelly was a fantastic two-way player. He was the best scoring defenseman of his era. Kelly won the Lady Byng Memorial Trophy three times with Detroit.

TERRY SAWCHUK   Goalie

- BORN: 12/28/1929   • DIED: 5/31/1970
- PLAYED FOR TEAM: 1949–50 TO 1954–55, 1957–58 TO 1963–64, & 1968–69

Terry Sawchuk was the best young goalie anyone had ever seen. In fact, Detroit traded star Harry Lumley to give Sawchuk more playing time. He rewarded the Wings with 56 shutouts over the next five seasons.

NORM ULLMAN   Center

- BORN: 12/26/1935   • PLAYED FOR TEAM: 1955–56 TO 1967–68

Norm Ullman challenged every opponent who had the puck, but few challenged him when he had it. Ullman's beautiful stickhandling made him a perfect linemate for high-scoring Gordie Howe.

ABOVE: Ted Lindsay and Gordie Howe

STEVE YZERMAN   Center

• BORN: 5/9/1965   • PLAYED FOR TEAM: 1983–84 TO 2005–06

Red Wings fans had gone nearly three decades without a Stanley Cup before Steve Yzerman arrived in Detroit. He would lead the team to three championships. On the way, Yzerman had one of the greatest seasons in history, with 65 goals and 90 assists in 1988–89.

SERGEI FEDOROV   Center

• BORN: 12/13/1969   • PLAYED FOR TEAM: 1990–91 TO 2002–03

After leaving Russia to play in the NHL, Sergei Fedorov quickly proved he was among the best centers in the league. During the NHL's **All-Star Game** festivities, he won the fastest skater and hardest shot contests. Fedorov was named winner of the Hart Trophy in 1993–94.

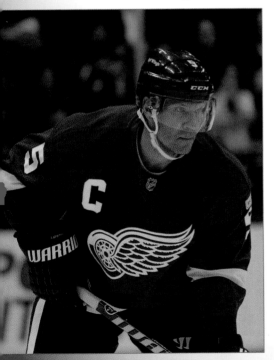

NICKLAS LIDSTROM   Defenseman

• BORN: 4/28/1970

• PLAYED FOR TEAM: 1991–92 TO 2011–12

Nicklas Lidstrom won the Norris Trophy as the NHL's top defenseman seven times and led the Red Wings to four championships. Few players could "read" the ice as well as Lidstrom. He could see an opponent's attack developing and stop it with a **check** or by stealing the puck.

BRENDAN SHANAHAN   Right Wing/Left Wing

- Born 1/23/1969   • Played for Team: 1996–97 to 2005–06

Detroit traded for Brendan Shanahan a week into the 1995–96 season. By the end of the year, the team had its first Stanley Cup in 42 years. Shanahan had an unstoppable **wrist shot** and was voted into the **Hall of Fame** in 2013.

PAVEL DATSYUK   Center

- Born: 7/20/1978   • First Season with Team: 2001–02

From the moment Pavel Datsyuk joined the Red Wings, Detroit fans knew he was something special. He seemed to know exactly when and where to pass the puck to give his teammates a great chance to score. Datsyuk scored 23 points in 22 games during the 2008 playoffs.

HENRIK ZETTERBERG   Center/Left Wing

- Born: 10/9/1980

- First Season with Team: 2002–03

Henrik Zetterberg was a smooth skater and a talented scorer who made the game look easy. Zetterberg scored the goal that won the 2008 Stanley Cup—and then signed the biggest contract in team history. In 2013, he was named captain of the Red Wings.

LEFT: Nicklas Lidstrom
RIGHT: Henrik Zetterberg

CALLING THE SHOTS

You know a coach is pretty good when they name the Coach of the Year award after him! Jack Adams was behind the bench for the Red Wings for more than 900 games starting in 1927. Adams had won two Stanley Cups as a player, so he understood what it took to play championship hockey. He was always very clear about what he expected from his players—and equally clear that he would get rid of anyone at a moment's notice. Some fans called him "Trader Jack." Adams also built the team's **farm system**, which produced the talent for three Stanley Cups in the 1950s.

Three Detroit coaches went on to win the Jack Adams Award—Bobby Kromm, Jacques Demers, and Scotty Bowman. Kromm was famous for whipping poor teams into championship form, and he nearly did so with the Red Wings in 1977–78. They doubled their number of victories from the year before. Demers was a genius when it came to getting players to blend their talents. He named Steve Yzerman the team's captain and was the first coach to win the Adams trophy two years in a row.

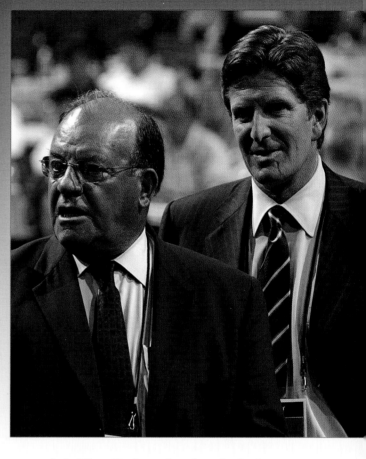

Scotty Bowman and Mike Babcock each led the Wings to the Stanley Cup.

Bowman was the coach who returned Detroit to its previous glory. He was behind the bench for Detroit's championships in 1997, 1998, and 2002. After the last Stanley Cup, Bowman strapped on a pair of old skates and joined his players as they took a victory lap with their trophy. He then announced that he was retiring.

Tommy Ivan, Jimmy Skinner, and Mike Babcock also led the Wings to the Stanley Cup. Ivan took over from Adams in 1947 and molded Detroit into one of the great clubs of the era. He guided Detroit to three championships. Skinner followed him and won the Stanley Cup in 1955. Babcock led the Red Wings to victory in 2008. He also led Team Canada to victory at the 2004 World Championships and in the 2010 *Olympics*. That made Babcock the first "triple-gold" coach in hockey history.

ONE GREAT DAY

Winning the Stanley Cup is one of the toughest tests in all of sports. Repeating as the NHL champions is even more difficult. By the 1990s, however, the Red Wings had already accomplished this feat twice, in the 1930s and again in the 1950s. Six days after winning the Stanley Cup in 1997, the team lost an important leader when Vladimir Konstantinov was badly injured in a car accident. He suffered brain damage and would never play again. Slava Fetisov was in the same crash. Luckily, he escaped unhurt.

All season long in 1997–98, the Wings missed Konstantinov. He had helped create great team chemistry. He also had a special talent for knowing exactly what would drive opponents crazy. The Red Wings sewed a special patch onto their sweaters with his initials and the word "Believe." They had the talent to win a second championship in a row. But fans wondered as the playoffs began, did the Wings have the heart to do so without Konstantinov?

The Wings gather around Vladimir Konstantinov after their championship in 1998.

Detroit answered this question by beating the Phoenix Coyotes, St. Louis Blues, and then the Dallas Stars. Each series was tough, but the Wings never gave up. By the time they reached the Stanley Cup Finals, they felt unstoppable. To no one's surprise, the Red Wings swept the Washington Capitals in four games.

Following their victory in Game 4, the Red Wings brought Konstantinov onto the ice in a wheelchair. They gave "Vlady" the Stanley Cup and then pushed him around the rink for a victory lap. He smiled widely and held up two fingers to make a "V" for Victory. Most of his teammates had tears in their eyes. Even the Capitals had to admire the moment. "That's outstanding what they did," said Washington coach Ron Wilson. "You'd only see that in hockey."

LEGEND HAS IT

WHICH RED WING MADE MORE MONEY IN ONE SEASON THAN AN ENTIRE NHL TEAM?

that Sergei Fedorov did. During the 1997–98 season, the Red Wings signed Fedorov to a new contract, which included a $14 million bonus. The following season, the Nashville Predators paid all of their players a total of $13.6 million. It was hard to argue that Fedorov was overpaid. Once, he scored all five goals in a 5–4 victory for the Wings.

: Sergei Fedorov became a rich man in 1998.

DOES IT TAKE A BRAIN SURGEON TO BECOME A SCORING CHAMPION?

LEGEND HAS IT that it does. At least, this was true for Gordie Howe. During the 1950 playoffs, Howe tried to check an opponent into the boards. Instead, he ended up fracturing his own skull. Howe was young and tough, but it was obvious something was very wrong as he staggered off the ice. He was taken to the hospital, where doctors diagnosed bleeding in his brain. They rushed Howe to the operating room and relieved the pressure before any damage was done. He was back on the ice the following season and won the NHL scoring title by 20 points!

WHO WAS THE FIRST PLAYER TO "HOIST" THE STANLEY CUP?

LEGEND HAS IT that Ted Lindsay was. After Detroit defeated the New York Rangers in double-overtime in Game 7 of the 1950 Stanley Cup Finals, the trophy was presented to team captain Sid Abel. Lindsay grabbed it from Abel and lifted it high above his head. He skated slowly around the rink, so all the fans could get a good look at it. Hoisting the Stanley Cup has been a hockey *tradition* ever since.

Imagine the thrill of scoring a goal to win the Stanley Cup in overtime—and not even seeing it! That actually happened to Tony Leswick in 1954. The Red Wings were locked in a fierce Game 7 battle with the Montreal Canadiens during the Stanley Cup Finals. The score was knotted 1–1 after three periods. The NHL crown would go to the first team that scored in overtime.

Leswick was an unlikely hero. His nickname was "Mighty Mouse" because he was one of the smallest players in the NHL. Leswick had spent much of his career playing for the New York Rangers, one of the worst clubs in the league. It was a gift when he was traded to Detroit.

The extra period was just a few minutes old when it was time for the Wings to get a fresh line on the ice. Leswick flipped the puck into the Montreal end, and then headed to the bench. Suddenly, the Detroit fans exploded in cheers. Leswick looked back to see the red goal light flashing. His teammates were leaping over the boards to celebrate. Leswick was stunned. Doug Harvey, Montreal's top

Tony Leswick kisses the Stanley Cup as Jack Adams and
teammates celebrate around him.

defenseman, had tried to knock the puck down with his glove.
Instead, he tipped it into his own net. Leswick had scored the
game-winning goal, and he was the only one in the building who
had not seen it!

TEAM SPIRIT

Detroit hockey fans are known for their loyalty. That is one reason the city has been called "Hockeytown USA." What Detroit fans are best known for, however, are their traditions. And the best-known is tossing octopuses on the ice. This began in 1952, when two brothers brought an octopus to Detroit's arena and threw it on the ice. Back then, it took eight wins to capture the Stanley Cup. The Wings won eight games in a row during the 1952 playoffs, and fans have been throwing the eight-armed creatures ever since.

Detroit's **mascot** is Al the Octopus. He is named after Al Sobotka, the man who cleans up the ice after fans throw octopuses on it. Sobotka also drives the machine that cleans the ice between periods. Al the Octopus lives in the rafters of Detroit's arena. He is raised up there before every playoff game.

LEFT: Al the Octopus is lowered to the ice before a game in Detroit.
RIGHT: Wings fans wore this pin in the 1950s.

TIMELINE

The hockey season is played from October through June. That means each season takes place at the end of one year and the beginning of the next. In this timeline, the accomplishments of the Red Wings are shown by season.

1932–33
James Norris buys the team and changes its name to the Red Wings.

1954–55
The Red Wings win their fourth Stanley Cup during the decade.

1926–27
The team joins the NHL as the Detroit Cougars.

1942–43
Johnny Mowers wins the Vezina Trophy as the NHL's top goalie.

1962–63
Gordie Howe wins his sixth scoring title.

Terry Sawchuk

Terry Sawchuk and Red Kelly starred for the Wings in the 1950s.

Red Kelly · defense
DETROIT RED WINGS

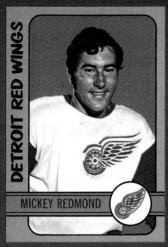

Mickey
Redmond

Pavel Datsyuk was
a star for the
2008 champs.

PAVEL DATSYUK
Center • Detroit Red Wings

1972-73
Mickey Redmond is the
first Red Wing to score
50 goals in a season.

2001-02
Dominik Hasek sets a
record with six shutouts
in the playoffs.

2007-08
The Wings win their
11th Stanley Cup.

1987-88
Jacques Demers wins
his second Jack Adams
Award in a row.

1996-97
Detroit wins its
first Stanley Cup
in 42 years.

2010-11
Nicklas Lidstrom
wins his seventh
Norris Trophy.

Nicklas
Lidstrom

FUN FACTS

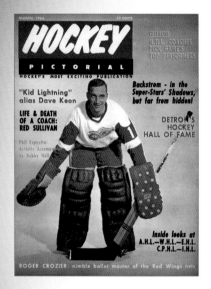

ROGER AND OUT

The Red Wings lost the 1966 Stanley Cup Finals, but Roger Crozier was so spectacular in goal that he won the Conn Smythe Trophy as MVP of the playoffs.

OLD TIMER

In 1997, the Detroit Vipers of the **International Hockey League (IHL)** signed 69-year-old Gordie Howe to a contract. He skated for one shift and became the first six-decade player in **professional** hockey history.

PASSING GRADE

In the 2002 playoffs, Dominik Hasek did something no goalie had ever done. With the Red Wings and Colorado Avalanche tied in overtime, Hasek fired a pass to Steve Yzerman. He fed the puck to Fredrik Olausson, who scored to win the game. Hasek got an assist—the first ever for a goalie in an overtime playoff game.

SWEDE VICTORY

In 2005–06, Detroit often played Nicklas Lidstrom, Henrik Zetterberg, Tomas Holmstrom, Niklas Kronwall, and Mikael Samuelsson at the same time. The "Swedish Five" also played together for their country in the 2006 Olympics—and led Sweden to a gold medal!

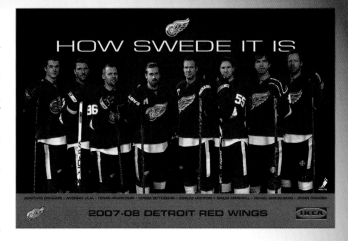

IN A FAMILY WAY

In 1949, Nelson Podolsky played his one and only NHL game for the Red Wings when Ted Lindsay had to sit out with an injury. Podolsky had been raised by Lindsay's parents in their Ontario home.

ZERO HEROES

Terry Sawchuk had 11 shutouts as a rookie for the Red Wings in 1950–51. Many fans thought no one would ever approach this record. They were wrong. In 1955–56, Glenn Hall had 12 shutouts in his first season in Detroit.

LEFT: Roger Crozier   **ABOVE**: By the 2007–08 season, the Wings had an even bigger Swedish presence on the team.

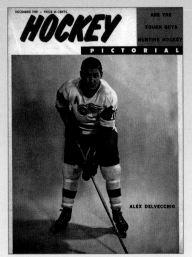

"You have very little time, you see very little, and everything happens really quickly."

▶ **STEVE YZERMAN,** *on why good instincts and reflexes are crucial in the NHL*

"The goals are nice, of course, but I've always taken a lot of pride in assists. It's a center's job to get assists."

▶ **ALEX DELVECCHIO,** *on the measure of a quality center*

"Take two seconds to see who's on the ice so you'll know where trouble might come from … and where help will be coming from."

▶ **GORDIE HOWE,** *on being aware of who else is on the ice before a line change*

"I guess I got rough because I hated to lose. It took me some time to learn the art of losing graciously."

▶ **TED LINDSAY,** *on why he had a reputation for "playing angry"*

"Gordie Howe wasn't just the best hockey player I've ever seen, but the greatest athlete."

▶ **BILL GADSBY,** *on his goal-scoring teammate*

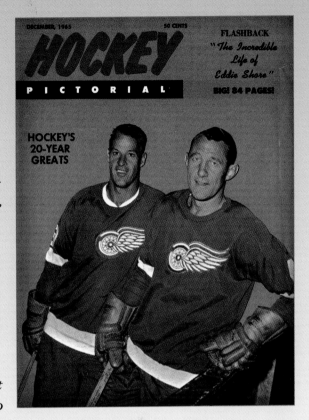

"I kept telling my wife, Gloria, to pinch me. I felt sure I was going to wake up and find I'd been having a wonderful dream."

▶ **SID ABEL,** *on winning the Hart Trophy as league MVP*

"Forward seemed a better position because a man can make more mistakes there and not be criticized as much for it. When you're on defense and someone skates past you, then you're the goat."

▶ **EBBIE GOODFELLOW,** *on the difference between the two positions he played for Detroit*

"I've been playing professional hockey for twenty years and this is the happiest moment of my life."

▶ **IGOR LARIONOV,** *on Detroit's 1997 Stanley Cup victory*

LEFT: Alex Delvecchio
ABOVE: Gordie Howe and Bill Gadsby

GREAT DEBATES

People who root for the Red Wings love to compare their favorite moments, teams, and players. Some debates have been going on for years! How would you settle these classic hockey arguments?

STEVE YZERMAN WAS THE BEST CAPTAIN IN RED WINGS HISTORY ...

... because he did the job longer and better than anyone else. Yzerman (   ) became captain at age 21 and held that position for two decades. No one in the history of North American team sports had served longer for one club. Yzerman took his captaincy seriously. Known mostly as a great skater and scorer, he became an excellent defensive player and led by example.

THINK AGAIN. NICKLAS LIDSTROM WAS DETROIT'S GREATEST CAPTAIN ...

... because he held the team together after their back-to-back Stanley Cups. Yzerman's teams were loaded with superstars and big-name talent. Most of those players were gone by the time Lidstrom took over. He not only led by example, Lidstrom also helped turn Detroit into a team that attracted players from all over the world. Under Lidstrom's captaincy, the Red Wings reached the Stanley Cup Finals three times and won twice.

BRENDAN SHANAHAN'S WRIST SHOT WAS THE GREATEST "WEAPON" IN TEAM HISTORY ...

... because of its power and accuracy. Shanahan (   ) was a veteran when he came to Detroit, and he knew the tricks of every goalie in the league. When "Shanny" had a clear shot at the net, he would wait for the goalie to give away his next move and snap off a shot an instant later. Detroit's opponents often focused their defense on stopping Shanahan.

NOT EVEN CLOSE. THE GREATEST WEAPON WAS GORDIE HOWE'S ELBOWS ...

... because they cleared space for him to shoot from anywhere on the ice. Like Shanahan, Howe had a powerful wrist shot, plus a great slapshot and a *lethal* backhand, too. He was able to take these shots at will because opponents were scared to get close to him. Anyone who tried to muscle Howe off the puck could expect a perfectly placed elbow-jab—and sore ribs for the next week!

T he great Red Wings teams and players have left their marks on the record books. These are the "best of the best" ...

Glenn Hall

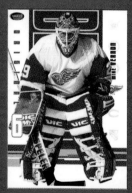

Mike Vernon

RED WINGS AWARD WINNERS

ART ROSS TROPHY
TOP SCORER

Ted Lindsay	1949–50
Gordie Howe	1950–51
Gordie Howe	1951–52
Gordie Howe	1952–53
Gordie Howe	1953–54
Gordie Howe	1956–57
Gordie Howe	1962–63

HART MEMORIAL TROPHY
MOST VALUABLE PLAYER

Ebbie Goodfellow	1939–40
Sid Abel	1948–49
Gordie Howe	1951–52
Gordie Howe	1952–53
Gordie Howe	1956–57
Gordie Howe	1957–58
Gordie Howe	1959–60
Gordie Howe	1962–63
Sergei Fedorov	1993–94

VEZINA TROPHY
TOP GOALTENDER

Norm Smith	1936–37
Johnny Mowers	1942–43
Terry Sawchuk	1951–52
Terry Sawchuk	1952–53
Terry Sawchuk	1954–55

CONN SMYTHE TROPHY
MVP DURING PLAYOFFS

Roger Crozier	1965–66
Mike Vernon	1996–97
Steve Yzerman	1997–98
Nicklas Lidstrom	2001–02
Henrik Zetterberg	2007–08

CALDER TROPHY
TOP ROOKIE

Carl Voss	1932–33
Jim McFadden	1947–48
Terry Sawchuk	1950–51
Glenn Hall	1955–56
Roger Crozier	1964–65

JAMES NORRIS MEMORIAL TROPHY
TOP DEFENSEMAN

Red Kelly	1953–54
Paul Coffey	1994–95
Nicklas Lidstrom	2000–01
Nicklas Lidstrom	2001–02
Nicklas Lidstrom	2002–03
Nicklas Lidstrom	2005–06
Nicklas Lidstrom	2006–07
Nicklas Lidstrom	2007–08
Nicklas Lidstrom	2010–11

RED WINGS ACHIEVEMENTS

ACHIEVEMENT	YEAR
Stanley Cup Finalists	1933–34
Stanley Cup Champions	1935–36
Stanley Cup Champions	1936–37
Stanley Cup Finalists	1940–41
Stanley Cup Finalists	1941–42
Stanley Cup Champions	1942–43
Stanley Cup Finalists	1944–45
Stanley Cup Finalists	1947–48
Stanley Cup Finalists	1948–49
Stanley Cup Champions	1949–50
Stanley Cup Champions	1951–52
Stanley Cup Champions	1953–54
Stanley Cup Champions	1954–55
Stanley Cup Finalists	1955–56
Stanley Cup Finalists	1960–61
Stanley Cup Finalists	1962–63
Stanley Cup Finalists	1963–64
Stanley Cup Finalists	1965–66
Stanley Cup Finalists	1994–95
Stanley Cup Champions	1996–97
Stanley Cup Champions	1997–98
Stanley Cup Champions	2001–02
Stanley Cup Champions	2007–08
Stanley Cup Finalists	2008–09

Jack Adams was the most important figure in the team's early years. After retiring as a player, he was hired by Detroit to run the club and led the Red Wings to seven Stanley Cups.

PINPOINTS

The history of a hockey team is made up of many smaller stories. These stories take place all over the map—not just in the city a team calls "home." Match the pushpins on these maps to the **TEAM FACTS**, and you will begin to see the story of the Red Wings unfold!

TEAM FACTS

1 Detroit, Michigan—*The team has played here since 1926.*

2 Chicago, Illinois—*Chris Chelios was born here.*

3 Minneapolis, Minnesota—*Reed Larson was born here.*

4 Kirkland Lake, Ontario—*Mickey Redmond was born here.*

5 Winnipeg, Manitoba—*Terry Sawchuk was born here.*

6 Calgary, Alberta—*Mike Vernon was born here.*

7 Melville, Saskatchewan—*Sid Abel was born here.*

8 Cranbrook, British Columbia—*Steve Yzerman was born here.*

9 Belfast, Northern Ireland—*Jim McFadden was born here.*

10 Njurunda, Sweden—*Henrik Zetterberg was born here.*

11 Pardubice, Czech Republic—*Dominik Hasek was born here.*

12 Pskov, Russia—*Sergei Fedorov was born here.*

Dominik Hasek

GLOSSARY

ALL-STAR GAME—The annual game that features the best players from the NHL.

ASSISTS—Passes that lead to a goal.

CHECK—A body blow that stops an opponent from advancing with the puck.

CONTENDER—A person or team that competes for a championship.

DECADES—Periods of 10 years; also specific periods, such as the 1950s.

DIVISION—A small group of teams in a conference. Each NHL conference has three divisions.

DRAFTED—Selected during the annual meeting when NHL teams pick the top high school, college, and international players.

ERA—A period of time in history.

FARM SYSTEM—The clubs that "raise" young players for an NHL team.

GENERATION—A group of people born and living at approximately the same time.

HALL OF FAME—The museum in Toronto, Canada, where hockey's best players are honored. A player voted into the Hall of Fame is sometimes called a "Hall of Famer."

HAT TRICK—Three goals in a game.

INTERNATIONAL HOCKEY LEAGUE (IHL)—The professional league that operated from 1945 to 2001.

LETHAL—Damaging or destructive.

LINE—The trio made up by a left wing, center, and right wing.

LOGO—A symbol or design that represents a company or team.

MASCOT—An animal or person believed to bring a group good luck.

MOST VALUABLE PLAYER (MVP)—The award given each year to the league's best player; also given to the best player in the playoffs and All-Star Game.

NATIONAL HOCKEY LEAGUE (NHL)—The professional league that has been operating since 1917.

OLYMPICS—An international summer or winter sports competition held every four years.

OVERTIME—An extra period played when a game is tied after three periods. In the NHL playoffs, teams continue to play overtime periods until a goal is scored.

PLAYOFFS—The games played after the season to determine the league champion.

PROFESSIONAL—A player or team that plays a sport for money.

ROOKIE—A player in his first year.

SHUT OUT—Held an opponent scoreless.

STANLEY CUP—The trophy presented to the NHL champion. The first Stanley Cup was awarded in 1893.

STANLEY CUP FINALS—The final playoff series that determines the winner of the Stanley Cup.

TRADITION—A belief or custom that is handed down from generation to generation.

VETERANS—Players with great experience.

WESTERN HOCKEY LEAGUE (WHL)—A rival league to the NHL, with teams in the western part of North America in the 1920s.

WORLD WAR II—The war among the major powers of Europe, Asia, and North America that lasted from 1939 to 1945. Canada entered the war in 1939; the United States followed in 1941.

WRIST SHOT—A shot taken by "flicking" the puck with a quick turn of the wrists.

LINE CHANGE

TEAM SPIRIT introduces a great way to stay up to date with your team! Visit our *LINE CHANGE* link and get connected to the latest and greatest updates. *LINE CHANGE* serves as a young reader's ticket to an exclusive web page—with more stories, fun facts, team records, and photos of the Red Wings. Content is updated during and after each season. The *LINE CHANGE* feature also enables readers to send comments and letters to the author! Log onto:

www.norwoodhousepress.com/library.aspx

and click on the tab: **TEAM SPIRIT** to access *LINE CHANGE*.

Read all the books in the series to learn more about professional sports. For a complete listing of the baseball, basketball, football, and hockey teams in the **TEAM SPIRIT** series, visit our website at:

www.norwoodhousepress.com/library.aspx

ON THE ROAD

DETROIT RED WINGS
19 Steve Yzerman Drive
Detroit, Michigan 48226
(313) 394-7000
http://redwings.nhl.com

HOCKEY HALL OF FAME
Brookfield Place
30 Yonge Street
Toronto, Ontario, Canada M5E 1X8
(416) 360-7765
http://www.hhof.com

ON THE BOOKSHELF

To learn more about the sport of hockey, look for these books at your library or bookstore:

- Cameron, Steve. *Hockey Hall of Fame Treasures.* Richmond Hill, Ontario, Canada: Firefly Books, 2011.

- MacDonald, James. *Hockey Skills: How to Play Like a Pro.* Berkeley Heights, New Jersey: Enslow Elementary, 2009.

- Keltie, Thomas. *Inside Hockey! The legends, facts, and feats that made the game.* Toronto, Ontario, Canada: Maple Tree Press, 2008.

INDEX

PAGE NUMBERS IN **BOLD** REFER TO ILLUSTRATIONS.

THE TEAM

MARK STEWART has written over 200 books for kids—and more than a dozen books on hockey, including a history of the Stanley Cup and an authorized biography of goalie Martin Brodeur. He grew up in New York City during the 1960s rooting for the Rangers, but has gotten to know a couple of New Jersey Devils, so he roots for a shootout when these teams play each other. Mark comes from a family of writers. His grandfather was Sunday Editor of *The New York Times*, and his mother was Articles Editor of *Ladies Home Journal* and *McCall's*. Mark has profiled hundreds of athletes over the past 25 years. He has also written several books about his native New York and New Jersey, his home today. Mark is a graduate of Duke University, with a degree in history. He lives and works in a home overlooking Sandy Hook, New Jersey. You can contact Mark through the Norwood House Press website.

DENIS GIBBONS is a writer and editor with *The Hockey News* and a former newsletter editor of the Toronto-based Society for International Hockey Research (SIHR). He was a contributing writer to the publication *Kings of the Ice: A History of World Hockey* and has worked as chief hockey researcher at five Winter Olympics for the ABC, CBS, and NBC television networks. Denis also has worked as a researcher for the FOX Sports Network during the Stanley Cup playoffs. He resides in Burlington, Ontario, Canada with his wife Chris.